SMOKING

THE

CITY

Poems by

BRYAN

McCARTHY

SMOKING
THE
CITY

McClelland and Stewart Limited   Toronto/Montreal

The Canadian Publishers
McClelland and Stewart Limited
25 Hollinger Road, Toronto 16

PRINTED AND BOUND IN CANADA BY
T. H. Best Printing Company Limited

To my mother

ACKNOWLEDGEMENT

For permission to reprint poems the author is
indebted to the editors of *Evidence*, *The Tamarack
Review*, *The Canadian Forum*, *Edge*, *Moment*, *Cataract*,
Prism (Montreal), and *The Bloody Horse*.

CONTENTS

Preface

I was born in London, England, in 1930. My mother had the English sense of social propriety. My father, Southern Irish, belched loudly and cursed like a trooper.

We were middle-class, yet lived in a working-class neighbourhood—an unusual circumstance in England. My parents told me not to mix with the local street-urchins and not to imitate their Cockney accents. The urchins, on their side, singled me out as fair game for their fists and taunts.

The most powerful influence in my childhood was the Catholic Church. Until my late teens I believed in heaven, hell, purgatory, transubstantiation, God, the Virgin Mary, and Papal infallibility. I believed that a miracle—something absolutely sacred—took place during each Mass. As an altar-boy I gave the priest bungling assistance in the rites prerequisite to this miracle.

Nuns and priests instructed me. The nuns, in their wimples and black robes, seemed sinister. I remember one aged Reverend Mother. As I answered her questions on the catechism I would stare fascinated at her left eye. It was filmy, creased across the ball, probably blind.

"Only one event is certain in this life," she would tell me, "and that is that some day you will die."

Catholicism gave me a sense of mystery—and of nightmare. It left me with a nostalgia for that state of inner integration which is purchased by absolute belief.

Although my parents entrusted my religious education to the Catholic Church, they were sceptical about the quality of the secular education provided by Church schools we could afford, and sent me to Protestant schools.

From the age of ten to eighteen, in the English equivalent of high-school, I drank up mathematics and science —a universe of order and reason, in contrast to other aspects of my life. Inevitably, the empirical-rational tradition conflicted with dogmatic Catholicism. For a time I tried to reconcile the two in terms of Thomist apologetics (instruction in which I received from a priest) but by the age of eighteen it was all up, and I ceased to believe in Catholicism.

At University, I became interested in left-wing politics. In 1950 I joined the Communist Party. My loyalty to the Party was always less than absolute. I began to meet people who had been in Stalinist forced-labour camps. From quite a different viewpoint, one fellow-student persistently argued with me:

"Can you give me one good reason why, during the revolution, I should not just stay at home and play billiards?" I gave him several, convinced nobody, and after a six-month stay, left the Party. In 1951, I graduated with a bachelor's degree in mathematics and physics.

Two years in the Royal Air Force followed. Then, from 1954 to 1956, I worked at a chemical plant in the North-East of England. The plant extended for miles. It was criss-crossed by railway tracks along which ancient, bell-clanging locomotives shunted. Overhead, thin frameworks bore aloft spherical or rectangular storage tanks. When the wind dropped and the air was damp, chemical fumes from the smokestacks came down and submerged us in dense, malodorous fog.

Like most people there, I worked without interest during the week and got drunk on Saturday night. On one such Saturday night in 1956, driving home fast from a dance with a party of drunks, I crashed my car. Earlier that week, a friend had written to me urging me to emigrate to Canada: I did.

Six days after arriving in Canada, I started work at Schefferville, fifteen hundred miles NNE of Montreal, on the Mid-Canada radar line. I saw a landscape like the surface of an alien planet: shallow worn hill after shallow worn hill receding to the bare horizon. There was no sign of anything human. From the top of a hill, I could see hundreds of lakes, unnamed, glittering, remote, alien. About six weeks later I was moved two hundred miles west, and spent the winter in a tent which I shared with a French Canadian. He went mad and tried to dispatch me with a crowbar.

I came down from the line with $2,500 in the bank and took a squalid room in Montreal, with the intention of staying there for a couple of years and writing a masterpiece. But I had no viewpoint. Life became phantasmagorical (see notes to the poem *Smoking the City*). I spent much of the time in bed, and left after two months.

In 1957 I attempted to sell encyclopedias on the West Coast of Canada. I ended up in Prince George, where I obtained gainful employment with the Forestry Service— going into the woods with a gallon tank of paint on my back, and putting blue dots on trees.

I then worked for a year on the *Prince George Citizen*. In 1958 I moved to Toronto where I became an editor with a chemical processing magazine. After five months I announced loudly that I was going to sacrifice Career for Art, quit, and moved to Montreal.

For the next seven months (1959), I lived on Unemployment Insurance money, and tried to write poetry. I was fortunate in meeting three Canadian poets whose influence on my poetry was then, and is now, crucial. They were Irving Layton, Al Purdy, and Milton Acorn. It seemed to me that they had forged a poetic idiom that was viable and modern. They'd ruthlessly purged all trace of Nineteenth Century romanticism from their work; in the grain and imagery of their verse was an awareness of modern life; and the language they used related to contemporary speech.

I lived on Crescent Street in a slummy block opposite the Champs Show Bar. I slept a lot and read existential philosophy. One day I encountered a mad old woman in the hallway who said, "There is a darkness in my room." This incident triggered me off into a poem (*Crone*, in this book) which was later published by Milton Acorn in his magazine *Moment*. It was the first poem of mine to be published.

I read less and slept more. Towards the end of the year I began to doubt my sanity. Hoping that I could save myself by honest toil, I got a job teaching delinquent and disturbed children. I lasted a month. At another and much better school for disturbed children, I got used to seeing teenagers make bungling attempts at suicide. I read: Miller, Orwell, Celine, Dostoyevsky, Kafka, Sartre, Mailer, Baudelaire, Mayakovsky, and the Beat writers Kerouac, Ginsberg, Corso, and Ferlinghetti.

Then in 1961 I met a bearded Beat poet from San Francisco. He convinced me that a 'scene' could be made in Montreal. He, I, and some others, including Milton Acorn, opened a coffee house called *The Place* on Stanley

Street in an old building which had previously been a whorehouse. While it lasted, *The Place* attracted every outsider east of San Francisco. The police, too, were frequent visitors. In December 1961, the bearded poet departed for points unknown with our capital, $500, and *The Place* folded. (It is now a parking lot.) I weighed 127 pounds. I had made the scene. I had (almost) had the scene. I opted for the middle way. I lived quietly, taught, and still teach, at a high school; and in 1964, married.

Montreal   BRYAN MCCARTHY
July 19, 1965

SMOKING

THE

CITY

Crone

The crone, clinging batlike to the wall
of the tenement-passage, said,
as I neared:

there is a darkness in my room.

I could have touched her face
yet her voice
was a lost, distant
cry . . .
the midnight scream
you pretend you do not hear
as you hurry home.

I backed away.
Madness had bored
holes for eyes
in her fumbling, wrinkled face.

Black holes, which drew, which drew,
for pity's sake like claws,
as if to tear
flesh from my shrinking, hoarded self.

She shuffles to her haunted room,
to boxes, heaps of rubbish, where the darkness
that never leaves her, shapes
creatures slavering to possess
her vacant soul. Beasts who watch
as she stares into the splinter of a mirror,
or coos to a baby made of bandages
wrapped round her dirty fingers.

She returns to her darkened room . . .
and somehow it is I
who tombed her there:
and now
          that certain darkness
enters my room.

City

i want mud, red mud.
i want
to squelch.

i'm tired of shaking hands with machines
and i'm afraid to look
at my own
magnetic fingers.
it's hot.
hot cars thrust
exhaust pipes
into my desert mouth
and elsewhere
if i give them the chance.
a very small, chic car
is lodged
in my gullet right now
as a matter of fact.
it's hot.

bombs are getting ripe
on the vine;
gardeners clank past me
with rustic
blowtorches.
and you, you sit tight:
what do you want?
a quarter
in your coinomatic head
i suppose. goodbye.
it's hot.
God
is mad, with the heat.
he's making
i don't know what he's making
he's making
an infernal racket.
i want out.
it's hot.
Please,
a pan of blue lake
and bring me mud
i want to sink my fingers

crotch-deep

in red mud.

Mr. Primfoot

The open-air shelter is grown over
        with thick-piled grass.
          "See," says Mr. Primfoot, "how nature hides
the ugly scars of war:
mellowed and grown-over who would guess
that these rounded humps once were stark
           emblems of terror."

Three yelling children appear:
"I shot you first," one says.

Crawling drops

If your tastes
             are sufficiently

                          dark
come with me to the dark vault

Echoes   a whispering
of drips   then
a face

      bulges
in your spotlight

All right   let's
             skip the dramatics
you're not really alarmed by this
leprotic
      scab of a face
      are you?

did you notice   though
                          his lips

        moved?

Look   they're grasping
those silver drops

    I don't think
he sees us
his eyes   staring out of
                          crusts

don't flicker   but   digressing
the drops   one slides in the
                          tumour of his lip

            were sought
                by all the scabbed folk
        who
            you've noticed
    in a sense
                live here

        That is   he
                    liked it
                    on his slab

But the
    crawling lies like slugs of mercury
    the
    NUMBNESS
                    is their first
                                gift
That
    racked torso
                dungeoned alive
                            in leprotic stone
their final

        benefit
this one tried
to get out
made it to the edge of his slab   before
                                becoming
set
  in his ways

Look at his face
                is it
                    familiar?

  Do you feel an odd
                    disinclination
                    to move?
8

Playing by ear

Who is this chalky fool
            droning through centuries?

Christ, it's
me

Like Whitman I (chalkdust)
think I contain
            multitudes

But find this less
            convenient
                    than apparently

he did

A bullet would
            improve the minds
of many of my citizens
and then the rest
perhaps

could get somewhere
YES but what about
new arguments! new wars!
new stalemates new
blockages!

Who said that?
            You're for the chop
                        my friend

But suppose (I'm soft) suppose

Look — the worst rogue of the lot
            flops boneless in the
                        dock
slips through my fingers with
            amoeboid plausibility

and under the door and down
the drain

or an idiot
plucks petals
simpering

                sad happy sad happy sad happy
                            DEAD
or it pours
piss-pots and angel feathers

oh god   will this babbling
Babel never
burst?

Yes, I guess, one day
it will

in the meantime, s'pose
I'd better
play it by ear
with a certain (nauseating)
quantum
                of good cheer

The window

From a tenement-window

cut
    in the black sky
he stares into a night
                    of low-grade crime

But actually he's a
                nice boy
and nobody hears
          when he mentions
          the
          cop

He drags you to the window, there's

no window you
          explain carefully
you point to the
          black mirror

you point to his white face in the
                black mirror

He agrees, yes he agrees
        but I do not recommend
                that you look
                        in his eyes

Better just
                fade out
                        NOW

he clicks the room dark but he
cannot resist he
cannot resist he
                twitches the forbidden
                blind
eyes the

        crack
his lips   bullets

So . . . he smiles
        softly

So . . . it's
    true

then DOWN in a haggish
          ecstasy of cackling
          tin-cans

the rusty corpse of fire-escape
                              drops
machine-guns mutter
under his smoking
              boots

everyone dead and gone but
police whistles   police whistles

big-bellied moronic
              buildings rush him

swerve
night extrudes
              a girder
under his riveting
              fear
and chasms   sirens

for a second
          enormous rays of light
              pin him
                    flat
                        to the wall

but he descends
         into night's

                  gutters

crawls until
         steel bars
press his jagged skull

The cop's eyes
         moisten
         as he draws
         his gun
the wrecked thing at his feet
         cannot make itself heard at all
above the interminable
boring argument
of the cylindrical
                  steel mouth

Arabesques

They stagger away from me, these
idiot lives

I see
     crooked fuses

   hissing
through loose dust

I see the heaps of bones
          dud
            death

And even the sun's an idiot

grinning at all the other skulls
          on this
                plain
                    of arabesques

They say that one of them
          got his
              clubbed boot

across the electrified
                    wire horizon
—you see that shining
heap?

Most
    fall nearer
they flump softly
            like gas-shells

But I
   shall
   make it

although my right foot's growing strangely
                                    obtuse

       I'll not
            swerve
                like
those   idiots
    I shall make it
                    yes

but what's this

vulture
        doing on my
                    wrist

and who is this
                    man
            with a steel

                    tripod?

choose your silhouette
            he says

but remember that
                    once chosen it's
chosen

The eye of the camera is
                    metallic
                            lust

He loads lead
            assumes
the black hood

Flattered, I fake an
                    opera of defiance

he crouches aims
                    he

                    smothers my breast

with red flowers

Smoking the city

I

The drunkard bedded comfortably
   in debts and broken glass
               —he's good for a laugh
or youthful
     genitals skewered
     with gilded ambition
           —that warms 'em up

the ringmaster now
          jackboots
               boastful whip
      PROUDLY PRESENTS
           an overcoat in the noonday sun
             it mutters
                 numbers
skips a crack among butt-ends in the sidewalk

we're ready we're ready he KNOWS
we're ready — NOW for the
death-
defying-drum-and-cymbal-
way-up-there
orgasmic

welder on a girder
drops two hundred feet into
the anonymous wicker basket
of a beautifully laundered
magnate

applause in castinets
from an audience

of
ghouls . . .

and you mon frère
have you not inhaled the city
have you not thanked god to feel
the coprophilia the necrophilia
take hold and sprout?

bedded comfortably
in your bombs and poison gas
have you not groped
for an hypodermic full of cops and bullets?

II

Once upon a time I lived in a cough
                          in a house in a lung.
What crap is this you ask?
        Good!   Fine!   Ask!
Shall I lash myself into a royal
and leonine rage
                          about nothing at all?
Very well.

The skins of the cheeks of the enormous
room
        were marvellously
                          pocked
and furthermore
                          breakfast was served
                                          every morning—
                          new-laid
                          blooded sputum
                                          on a silver salver

The landlady, a hushed whisper, was to be found
                at the bottom of the stovepipe
                                that went through my floor
                in a huge nest of rags and fishbones
                with her lord
                          the colossal
                          cough

boast!   of course I boast—
and wouldn't you, wouldn't you
peacock too, if you had my youth my
magNIF-
icent youth
              behind you?

              .   .   .

MA whyn't you get that
                        yellow stuff outa yr ears?
(My ear grasped
                  the stovepipe —
   And I was limber
                    nonchalant as a nude
                                        in a Buffet-room
   with a bed
               constructed of prison bars. . . .
   But I tried to escape I tell you
      plotted
             struck
                    again   again)

Grease the pan ma
            I wanneat
      continued the lordling

Whyja lie around in
         THAT all day?

White nerves grew out of my ear-drum
                     and ramified the lung
And the old, the venerable
         Cough one day declared
       I'm hone a da HACKEY
      da HACKEY
            da HACKEY

by now
       my eyes
       were closing fast
and bombs, like salty
      tears but

I struggled
           staggering across the blazing desert
           of bed

(call it, if you wish,
       a sentimental distaste
            for premature burial
    but truly I tried
            to stay awake)

cumbersome were my eyes
              lumbering that dark room

and men with hand-grenades and knives
             stood over me
prussic waves of clink
                        filled the bottle-room
                        next door

my long fingers stroking

a dirty hypodermic
                  of puns
                        and blasphemies

with a very
          detached
                  smile
I watched blue eyes on books on electric lines
until a cop bubbled upwards
out of my down-going nostril

they told me to admire him
they told me to build
they told me
to carve the ooze
into absolute shapes

and I tried to tell you!
I hacked!   I chopped!

then woke
in my stovepipe's
                nihilistic
                        whisper

            .   .   .

Yea Yea
        the city burns!
I drag it into subterranean
                        lungs
like holy
marijuana

Spinster

I put down
her oval
photograph
                and suddenly find myself
in a movie
            of forgotten clichés

you know
            an ancient
            wedding dress
                            hobbles down
                                dark stairs—
and dark corridors and flames
and scourging
clocks . . .

It's late.
I confess I'm
spooked—
Dickens I suppose—
anyway I keep

                     quiet
                          and the sepia photograph
stares.

She was flower-like

luminous

but in those
haunted eyes

     already
that first
fatal

turning away
of a dark intelligence

that fatal
turning back

Spider

So I'm in this tavern growing smoky and lachrymose,
eight possible paths, none of them too long,
all of them twisted like the legs of a bashed
spider—
         and eight identical selves
         creep down these paths
         which radiate from my table

Suddenly crafty I
clip off
a path

      it twitches
      in a pool of beer

      at the feet
      of a white-haired

      drunkard—
      but the bastard
      doesn't notice

After the fifth quart my
             distended brain
        lurches
above me
on seven
        rickety legs

The dripping mass
makes it

        to the pissoir

The robot

It's
   plugged in
         to an income—
Some bastard presses a button. Watch.

It gets up
very carefully not
         waking
           the wife.

Once, just as the thing was hooking me

I looked
steadily
    into its eye.

Believe it or not

      that neon
      flickered.

The search

Some
     go on the road
               to find it;
burrow
      their own collapsing
                brains
to get at it.

But
   last night
after my
     seven winters
               in the woodwork
it came
of itself.
It seemed to be red angel's wings.
They whacked
            and battered me
then went.

31

And now
       the usual
              steel dawn
cuts cracks in your face
                   my friend
         and in
              this building.

Better not go too close to the walls,
better keep
       the straightest
              of straight faces.

If some of the cracks
            aren't really there, remember
others
    are INVISIBLE

Let's agree
       we're stuck
            in an ancient
                 web;

what
should I do, do you think?—
     struggle
         or rave
            go mad

tear angels
      flaming
           out of my beard?
On this

      argument
      continues.

So does the search.

Postscript for Terese

I'd just crawled
to the bottom of my pit.
"Shit-snake," you hissed,
peering down at me. I knew
I was part of you then, honey.
Understand?
"Weakness," you hissed, "weakness! Do you
want to be a failure? Is that what you want?"
No my dear.

I want to be tit-fed on angel's milk.
Then I lie back, not saying:
"—think I couldn't hustle my sweet ego
any day of the week
with the rest of the Bards?"
Should I? I wonder. Slingshot the bores? Ah, shit,
I'm crawling into the shape
of a new hypothesis.
Weak. That's it. I'm weak.

And now my plasticene eyes are being
gouged out by the young lady who also
twists and stretches my jaw like bubble-gum.
Ecstasies. Illuminations. Explosions
of pink bubble gum.
You admire your handiwork:
"NOW DO SOMETHING"
—there's almost hope in your voice.

And, hell, I look at it, really look at it,
quite startled. Shall I climb the slimy slope?
Hood, puff, poke out my tongue? All that?
But . . .
what would be the point?
I don't put it to you like that, it's
already dragging you I know, dragging you enough.
Instead, with (prodigious) courage
I click-shut my golden eyes
and with reserved colossal strength
coil myself into the very bottom of the pit
for another cosy millennium at least.

In the red desert

Motionless, it hurls up chrome
in front of me:
a steel-armoured
insect
many times the size of a man.

—beaked idol
squatting **erect**
like a praying mantis.
Not moving.
Catatonic in some dream
of clocks and falling cities.

I crawl
on the lethal page of its calculations;

begin to thrill
sensing the gleaming soar and rise of it

knife-jaws, hooking at the sun,
forelegs
murder-probed.

—a flashing electrical dream
and myself
meshing in circuits;
myself, under magnifying eyes
that bulge like aircraft-gun-turrets.

Then, in the dream, a tremor.

A tremor—

and slowly, delicately,
slowly and delicately as a cracksman
opening a safe
with silken fingertips
the glittering monster
bares its greenish dome of intellect
to the torturing sun,
and slowly, delicately
pushes in
one searching surgical probe, and then another
into the gristled nerve-cells.

Very rarely, as the sun
crawls over metal
the round head droops, the mandibles gape.
A million furnace-mirrors
daze compassion out of my head.

❋   ❋   ❋

A sick convulsion twists and shakes the monster.
It topples:
Legs jerkily grope the sky for footholds
but the probes, obsessed
still rend and tear the brain . . .

sick and trembling
I turn away from the dying
gleaming wreckage
and clutch
my burning skull.

Going down

I began to sink.
Very slowly, at first.

Then, in the grimy slush of conversation, I was brutally
hauled down a manhole by proletarians in black rubber
uniforms.

In the pestilent light, I nodded curtly at Orwell and Miller
and hurried along a passage, gut-slick, which twisted to left
and brought me to the congested tedium of a love-affair.

I gripped her ceiling, I tell you, like
a cockroach, while she lay on a greasy couch of sponges,
shrugging her eyebrows, and munching a kind of porrage
           made
of my poems.

For fourteen days we heaved sex-symbols and
           sherry-glasses over
chessboards, or rolled ponderous arguments of brass in the
basement—

Inevitably sinking up to the groin in intriguing, squalid,
ooze.

But at last, one midnight, I carried out her heavy, ticking,
anarchist bomb-soul, on a pointed shovel, and buried it
under a heap of recriminations.

The conflagration was beautiful and lasted for days.

I continued to sink:
subsided through three kingdoms, through my mother and
        father
through modes and infinities.

Apprehensive at all times of certain urchins, who
        brandished
musical instruments.

One day, strolling cautiously along the dock, with a blood-
soaked parcel of bandages thrust under my trench coat
I noticed a tiny door:

In a second
I was safe

Inside my own head
            staring at sea-monsters
            through a kind of port-hole.

Spring whimsy

What a fey, whimsical sort of a day it is!

A poodle rushes a spike-tailed pheasant in the park.
Poodle?
That gives me
Paris

a whangy cane twanging along the boulevards;
the Eiffel Tower popping out champagne-corks

It's a Maurice Chevalier sort of a day
with a breeze
frisking my hair.

I foresee light Dufy summers
of blue and yellow brush-strokes
on a cartridge-paper sky

and other whimsies:
Pink boats tied up with twisted
liquorice hawsers
and my poems, light pink feathers
blowing out of my hand

and parachuting
down
      past pink-owly faces
of 1920 geranium-window-box

She

 I cannot see her
for hallucinations
of pink champagne
and spun-glass slippers.
I do not believe in her.
Slyly I fish for her
in silver mirrors.
Where does she live?—
Beyond the corner of my eye.
She is a smile
beyond censors
and the censors of censors.
I do not believe in her.
Slyly I fish for her
in silver mirrors.

Moloch

He straps his son to a
sacrificial machine
crams the cheap cigar-ash
of contract into his soul,
and the huge
           thunderous
                     angel-wings
   of majesty and horror

he locks away in a tiny safe.

What are you Moloch?—
my own mediocrity mirrored,
my grossest, lack-love self stretched out
like heavy rubber
in the black sky?
Moloch; the coarse-lipped;

exhaling thick smoke into the bright eyes of girls,
leading us on past easy deals to Dachau—
yet Moloch, Moloch you're the absolving god, you
alone forgive, forgive us anything—
No wonder we heave you high above the world
on bruised shoulders.

—O I've seen the city saint smash out
from neon solitudes
and thong his wrists to your thrashing-machines
joyous, weeping;
I've seen the anchorite tumble down
from his absolute girder
and vanish
with legerdermain readily understood;

Yea, crushing Moloch, you absolve, you bless us.
Yea, Moloch, yea, your yoke is light.

8:30 a.m. bus line-up

our immense souls
  have shrunk
          into something about the size
of a smoked oyster—
    something small, fleshy
and wincing
peering out
        through eyeslots
in the cockled metal cans
of propriety.

don't worry, neighbour:
I won't thrust my coarse hand
    into your snail-sensitive soul—
I won't batter your rusted legalities—
I too
    observe
    the pacts
        I too
am waging secret freezing uncanny war

of silence
          against you

and sometimes, friend, I too
          grope and lunge
in the cold dark
of my cockled tin-can.

look—
part of me says we're
     quietly stolidly
mad

what? shall I bust
out? hot-kiss
          kiosks?
casually cosh the passer-by
                    with leaded love?
make crash the driver's jawbone to the floor
               with a savage
                         "good morning"?

craftily I eye
enormous Tuts—
the guards with guns and clubs
          at all the senses.

nobody moves.
we are mad.
catatonic—
    welded into our madness.
we are mad
we are mad

only the little children
   are not mad

   —born amid the falling
                  snowflakes
capering rosy-
cheeked-delight

       or weeping

weeping like stars . . .

The facts of life

Sometimes they
                floor me.
Like this thirteen-year-old boy I
tutor (five bucks)
                this flop-eared
nursery hare
                who asks, with a touch
of mockery
                "Sir, why aren't you married?"
and answers chuckling
                "No money I'll bet."

Identity
                mislaid
                        I

grope soft tentacles
                        about that rather

sharp-edged
question,
give up, stretch
    tall as an easel
my face white
with innumerable sums.

And actually
    boom to myself
    God, when I was thirteen . . .

fearing to see
Pooh-bear
   with a pot
      of nerve-gas
or making believe with a live
        bazooka.

This boy—
knows
"investments," yet,
to me

kites the word
   over purple
      crayon-trees.
Or have I been hoaxed?—

"First," he says, "I'll buy an apartment-block—"

And then leans back, not turning a whisker.

And of marriage:

"Guess I would
  like a few little rascals
  round the place—

and we'd live in the country

and know what—I wouldn't
register the births

and none of us would ever

      (O upsidedown green cockatoos!)

go to school."

To a north-american matron

Not nature
        but surely some raving madman
                    with a dagger
        and the jagged imagination
                of picasso
           hacked and slashed
         those zig-zags
              in your face
or hammer crazed
        your porcelain youth

Not growth not grief
no process as of gourd or sunlight or leaf

      could have
      cracked
         and strangulated
         your voice
             to a parrot-screech

could have shoved you to the safe distance
of a gaudy
              crocodilian mask
              at which we stick out sharp steel
                  tongues—

Poor woman
wretched fate
              you
did not will it
              your sons
flee you
        scattering bouquets and birthday cards

Poor woman
with arms like javelins
                      raised to caress
              menacing that charity
              which alone could save you—

That's it kierkegaard

That's it kierkegaard
      that's your
20th century either-or:
  either lam it along that lean and lonely
                           tightrope
             over the looneybin
or get flattened between
two sheets
        of thick plate glass
—shoved under the door
of the sales-office manager:

For the little grey men are moving in
my friends
         new york london moscow
spreading like
cold-wet-concrete-lava erupting
insurance blocks
         with a million square eyes;

not too many leaves and shrubs

                          my friends

        but

            cars cars cars cars

            & metaphysics of

                      dual exhaust-pipe

spreading like chancrous steel

better get out

better get out

            little grey men

           bombs—no wonder

            holiday magazine

           spreading—no wonder

           forests of vertical kleenex

better get out good friends

          or get

                right in

(find a

          parenthesis

      in the age

            and insert yourself

    damn quick

Hating the city

1.

Walking the streets
I saw men fearful
gibbering behind
blank faces;
saw living hands and eyes
viced
in a complicated scream
of metal;
I saw men sick
with anger, sick with
envy, sick with
machinery;
jabbering chromium masks;
I saw dead slaves
shackle their children's children's limbs
to the piston-rods
of avarice;

I saw black shadows
vague forms in nighttime perspectives
of doubt;
I stared up
at paper pinnacles;
I saw
        ashen faces

hurtling towards me like purgatorial sleet.

2.

Hating the city, I myself began to change:
my laugh
had an edge now.
The wryback, the amputee on six-inch
wooden stumps, yielded
new, perverse humours.
Trees were unreal
but at night
real cop-cars screamed.
My mind became
a machine of revenge
shaking itself to bits.
My flesh
striated
to bullets.

With a very strange smile
I heard men talk of God amid churchly
money-clink;
I saw men who might have been intellectual heroes
play panel-games to profit hucksters.
I saw the campus poets
sipping critical tea from chinese cups
dreaming guggenheims
as their flesh
crumbled.
(They told me of "tenure"
    and of
            "point of view.")

  Yet always I saw the brief, zesty flame-burst of spirit:
a child holding its ear in the cold and laughing;
the disorganized mind leaping at a truth.
And the flame-bursts of jubilation:
        the after-hours
        jazzman
the one-night stand.

(and always the flame extinguished:
    the hurried departure with a quick glance
    over the shoulder:
    always the fuzz-fear.   )

Walking the streets I heard
foundations crack.

I saw buildings go down

before they were built

On a high lean girder

On a high lean girder
                    in the black sky
I wait
      for an angel
to come with her soft copper brush.

For decades I erected
                    this structure
yet feel I am

              no nearer the sun—

my spanners are dull, hands
dull, mouth dull;

another framework
of girders
nearby
        soars up—up—
into the blinding sun.

At night I faintly discern a man up there
adjusting stars
riveting moon-rays.

But I—
     I must wait
  for an angel to alight
on my girder

with her brush
of soft copper.

Green bottles

Drunk—passing out—I
suddenly see
           —six bottles!
As never before
              bottles—!

Motionless!
        Violent!
              Shining!
          Electrical!
Sputtering a light in my
                dungeon—

                  brain—!
Just six green bottles—
              Possessed!   Unbearable!
  Levels of ice and
              energy!

Medieval!
Motionless!
Eternal
            essence!
Eternal white essence
                    of

                    bottle-glass!
                    bottle-glass!
Flash!—
of eternity's camera

cuts out black——

West-coast lotos

    Fresh, deep-sea air with a
whiff
     of lotos;

    masts like bamboo reeds of
      neat little red-or-white boats for week-end sailors
      on blue sea

    my god
    this is the life

    westerly wind tows darker-blue riffles
    across the blue bay from

         smoke-blue mountains with
         wild-scribbled zig-zag peaks

maybe this really
is
  it—
        thighs
in hot sand
head against a log of driftwood

no good no evil no ugly
  machinery above the eyes—my world—

all fresh and singing and blue
  as the first brush-strokes of a watercolour

two slender negro children in tiny blue
            bathing trunks
                        splash in the blue water

"Watch me!"—ducks under for five long seconds

            bobs up

Part of me opens perfumed
  petals
        in the sun

the rest
        mercifully
sleeps . . .

Power failure

heads spinning like pineapples
on slow blue turntables
Coltrane's sax shimmering
snarling in your sex
everyone hugging jigging jabbering
down
    in that hot-lit

           yellow cellar—

and then
without
introduction
with a wham
        inaudible
to all
but special ears
it

strikes

there's a flash an arc-
    blue flash a smell of scorching
and in that lean arc-blue light
    the stomping
            stomping finger-snapping
                            dancers

    go suddenly rigid
            silhouetted
                in attitudes
                of jagged metal

and you   still moving
eyes brimming with electrical blue light
    slowly
        duck
            under an iron
                            arm
                            rusted
talon raking your cheek
step into a forest   of jagged steel

and by that light   by that lean blue flashing light
    know each
glittering cog-wheel eye's each bronze-
            goggling socket in the round skull's
                welding you
                            into its own
            steel forest

O when
   it strikes when
   it strikes your best heart-clasping friend's
   burnt black
                to a twisted guttered
      semaphore you can't decipher
you move from black figure
      to black
          rigid
            ragged figure
touching listening groping . . .

                        .

snapped
back
      by the fat yellow click you
          jive again in the japering room
but it's not the same
in that hot cellar

            there are distances
                            chasms
in handclasps

                  and part of you
shuffles away
                  through that
      steel forest

Poem for reading

This is not a poem I read
very often.
It's not a poem at all but a kind of visual
accident.
At the same time it's a very
mysterious poem—
I want you to observe
                    very carefully
                    exactly what happens
and to observe
            your own
            interpretation of this.

Look: a ten dollar bill—
it's genuine—no deception.
And here's
        a box of matches.

Now observe
your feelings
          carefully
                    as you
                    watch me.

❋   ❋   ❋   ❋   ❋   ❋   ❋   ❋

          (The reader burns the bill)

❋   ❋   ❋   ❋   ❋   ❋   ❋   ❋

Good.
Now watch your feelings, watch
them
very carefully:
                    some of you are thinking
"marvellous" or
"idiotic" or "don't know" or
"exhibitionist" or
                    "he can't be short of money"
     or many other things
     or all of these at once;

all of which thoughts
as you by now
may realize
are
     accidents.

You were probably not bored by all this
unless you were very
                        sophisticated
at the time;
but in either case
your response

was an *accident*.

Portrait of myself doing good

                batwingy tenement-passage
where the air
                creeps up behind &
jumps you with its urinated blanket.
I twist myself into tatty
tight
        umbrella of will-to-do-good
and rap
    on her door;
aaaaaaaaah
mephistopheles
                what is it   what is it   I
don't know seems to be whacking
me in face with a hundred decapitated
chicken wings I desperately
grip my thin prim smile now I
actually its just incredible din of herself
shrieking at baby   phone shrilling   her eyes

running up and down the wall and me
skittering into a billion bits   but now
slowing getting a grip
on myself
again.

Now I'm cool. I make sharp
salvation army eyes at her prod out
five thin sticks of chalk she
clutches buzzard's nest of hair
shuffles inside in what was once
a dressing gown.

"Oh god I must look a wreck a sight, you
don't mind do you you don't mind—"

Fixedly
I stare
at a fry-pan full of cat-turds
by the door.
This evening
I am a saint
& have come
to succor the afflicted—

"You don't mind coming you
don't mind coming do you it's so
creepy alone excuse my back my hair's
in a mess oh eddy stop it
stop it—"

Baby sleds in on midnight
piss-pot.
"No no no of course I don't mind—"
—feeling shitty miffed and mad already

at endless strings of lies ripped out of my flesh
feeling the whole chaotic room grip hold of me
rushing me out of myself to crapulous madhouse
beginning at the back of my head
to gibber.

"I'm not a good mother. I'm letting him down—"

Baby howls in box of garbage—
Curtains swoop in like ragged bats—

"What? What? What? Why you're the perfect mother
Joan, little bastard'll grow up
blade-straight and clean—no
queer or nut-case he—"

My pity siphons off from her and plashes me
with its trunk of mad elephant;
ecstatically she strums the steel
belly-guitar of my knackered nerves: ach—

ach
she's coming at me from all sides!
rambling up and down this vault of junk and dead cats!
she tears long fish-papers out of her hair and eyes
Oh fuck you fuck you fuck you I screech
to my prostrate ear
my flow of sour sympathy cuts out with a glottal glug

with a glottal glug
cuts off

eyes
        twitch and scurry
no way out!
never never again will I play the saint
I will not kiss sores

oh god
must I forever caress and soothe this madwoman?—
I caress   I soothe
                    ——then inspiration
grab her cunt

Shrieks she and giggles coy and freezes rigid:
"Oh stop it stop it bryan
    oh stop it stop it stop it stop it stop it—!"

  of concrete is her pubis made
and she will never move
feet slabbed rigid to the creaking floor

I bow from the waist
with a brisk and courteous click
    proffer

    five thin sticks of chalk
to her statue-of-liberty hand—

skid off away down chilly splintering streets
she dwindles to a piteous case
I swivel
OH NO I roar
I do not turn back

                    fuck that

Michael

1.

Suddenly scared I open the door
                    no one
then
        this shimmering individual
                    wavers in, iridescent
                                        a
lustrous bubble
            wafted in the zephyr of your unexpressed
                                        wish
our whispers
            urge him into corners
hearts pounding we hold
                    our breath
but you've only to let your
                    brain
                        die

and he's there

             glistening
       metal
              in the centre

agreeable   charged   electrical
                                    yet
recedes
    from
            the lie-exhaling hand

& nobody

      grasps him

2.

Already I begin to feel a delicious
                             fear
I foresee these
           bubbles
           will multiply
I see their electrical gleam
           in
           smiles
                I don't quite get
      sputtering blue in the
                  edge
                      of madness

one day

      these
      will come

      barging round corners
      massive
      glistening

      shimmering
      with destrudo

and all the hosted
            trumps
               of plutonium

      will sound—

The Man with the Terrible Green Eye

In a neighbourhood
    of hurrying legs and wheels
he loafs;

he smiles
sardonically, lolls
        against the wall

        like one
of those insolent
key-chain-swinging gangsters

you sometimes see
        in an old movie:
but it's not

a key that he swings
in morning
        sunlight

it's that secret
eye of his
    that he swings

and cleverly catches.

Across the street
spike heels
    clack in and out

of the Bank,

and manicured eyebrows
frown
      vivid with purpose.

The man with the terrible eye
    arrogant and at ease
in wide lapels,

smiles strangely,
touches a flat grey building
with questioning fingers;

then, grin
bared,
screws in that terrible

glass-green eye,
watches
      cracks

branch out
in buildings and faces,

in white
gasping faces;
sees ladders

swoop to see-saws
teetering
   over midnight

chasms, boss
  at one end
office-boy at the other.

And in his skull the
ice-pick-heels, faster,
crash like guns

and he's marching, marching the flaming
cracking streets, the flaming falling
debris

of arms and legs—
he breaks smoking
walls, flames

lick his
bared grin, and
      with a shout

blasts the last safe-door
  of attachment:

then suddenly he's in a dark place,
alone, in a vast
terrifying

silence.

Shaking fingers crawl
to the blazing eye
    and wrench it out.

He stands
    head bowed
shivering
    in golden sunlight;

in the composed
simple sunlight
of a busy neighbourhood morning.

The new man

so i begin to make this phoney personality
eagerly it steps away from me its vacant hungry eyes
     bugging with
joy like flashing press cameras
it hefts weight   it bulges with creampuff muscles
and the voice springy and resonant fits well into
     microphones
girls look up to it dazzled: I hardly know you they say
digging my new voice my new
muscles &
meanwhile in a somewhere dark the sneering aging

me-master sits
somewhat wrinkled and bluish fragmenting into
cigar-ash chalk dust
blue and luminous as herring skins
and curved as an s-hook
all right old man all right you crumbling
crapulous creeping jesus

i will be that
it
that phoney
it, as you call it you
liar: old man i me it
glare at you through
thick plate glass quite
safe already from your gothic curses
talk of humility and love:
hah he withers and crumbles and as he
withers my muscles grow young and
hard and my eyes

        flash

        flash

        flash

NOTES

The Window – Page 12

The prophetic outsider, from his vantage point, sees life as a routine of unheroic crime.

He senses the unwitting hostility of society (the 'Cop') towards that creative imagination which gives his life meaning.

He tries to get others to look through his personal window, but is told that what he sees is merely himself, reflected in the "black mirror" of his own imagination. Therefore he "smiles / softly" when, again alone, he rediscovers his vision.

Images of pursuit follow, and, finally, the outsider is killed. The "boring mechanical argument" is that of society against the prophet.

Arabesques – Page 16

When values collapse, life is flattened to a desert of absurdity. People's lives become inane arabesques tracked in sand. These tracks resemble winding fuses that sputter and hiss towards the emphatic non-explosion of "dud-death."

A myth survives that someone once broke free of absurdity—got his boot across the "electrified / wire horizon." Each of the absurd creatures nurses such a hope for himself, though, like the protagonist of this poem, he may view the hope ironically.

Confronted by cameraman Death, the protagonist chooses his destiny, his "silhouette," and in that irrational act, achieves ambiguous glory.

Smoking the City – 19

The imagery of Part II is based upon my experiences in a squalid rooming house on City Councillor's Street, Montreal, where, early in 1957, I attempted to write short stories. Nothing I wrote satisfied me. I became inert: my frame of mind, bizarre.

A large iron bed, the "bed constructed of prison-bars" of the poem, dominated my room. The frame stood out, black and gaunt as a Buffet painting, against cracked walls.

Each morning I'd find the landlord's "new-laid / blooded sputum" in the half-blocked toilet. The landlord was a hoarse, shambling wreck. "I'm hone a da HACKEY," is his hoarse version of "I'm going to the hockey." When he coughed the whole house seemed to cough, racking itself out like a diseased lung. In my bizarre frame of mind, this huge cough took on an identity of its own—became the "lord" of the poem. The "lordling," his son, was one of the aggressive, aggrieved, lost teenagers that the modern city spawns in such quantity. His satiric thrusts, quoted verbatim in the poem, gave a just picture of his slovenly mother.

I grew withdrawn, and my contact with the human race dwindled to landlady's conversations which were conducted to my ear by a stovepipe that came through my floor from the kitchen beneath. As

"My ear grasped / the stovepipe," listening became a way of holding on to reality.

In the "bottle-room" adjoining mine, a noisy drunkard lived, who, to my hallucinated ear, would stack his entire room with clinking bottles. As I dozed, the sound became sinister "prussic waves of clink." Everything was seen in this nightmarish light, "Men with hand-grenades and knives / stood over me," referring to a recurrent nightmare of that time.

Four years later, I used these images to express my feelings about the modern city, which appears to me to be: evil, surreal, dislocated, bizarre, alienating—dreadful, but marvellously dreadful.

The Man with the Terrible Green Eye – 80

The ladders are value-systems of any kind—e.g. that system which regards "boss" as above "office-boy." When such a ladder falls, boss and office-boy see-saw on it as equals—the question of rank having become meaningless.